HOW TO START & GROW
YOUR OWN LAW FIRM

COOPER SAUNDERS

MILLER LEONARD

WISEGUYS

CONTENTS

PART I

STARTING A LAW FIRM

BY MILLER LEONARD

INTRODUCTION

If you are confused about how to open your own law firm, join the club. This book aims to help you solve the problems you face in opening your own law firm. Unlike many books, there are two authors of this book. One is a lawyer, and the other helps firms market and brand themselves.

This book is designed to give you concrete suggestions on how to make your dream a reality. It is a practical guide. Here you will not find the Socratic method of law school.

Why is it so hard to find help in starting a law firm? Even though the law is a profession, it is not, on the whole, a profession that sees the world with an abundance mindset. Most lawyers and law firms view the world with a scarcity mindset. This is a huge mistake.

This book is designed for more than just those ready to start their own firm. It is also meant for those with it as a career goal to be their own boss and run their own law firm. For those who aren't yet ready, the planning starts now. And for those prepared to go, this book will give you the help you need.

As you read through this book, remember that owning and

running a law firm is a mix of the profession of law and the business of law. Most lawyers need to improve in the business of law. Cooper has excelled in the business of law, and he wants you to succeed. You can have no better teacher.

It's time to make your dreams a reality.

CHAPTER ONE: WHEN

The law is a profession. You attend three years of law school and, upon graduation, must take and pass the bar to practice. Despite improvements in law school, a person is not prepared to practice law upon graduation.

Medicine has addressed the issues of preparing Doctors by implementing residencies. The law has no such requirement. But it is wise for a lawyer to spend several years learning the practice before opening a law firm.

How long should someone practice before they open their own firm? 3 – 7 years is a reasonable period. Each practice area differs, so adjust according to your chosen area. But after 3- 7 years, a lawyer has a good amount of practice under their belt, and they usually handle cases independently from inception to conclusion.

If you are in law school or a new lawyer, use the time you are studying law and learning the profession to gain better insight into the business of law. Just because you aren't ready to implement the strategies, blueprints, and systems you will discover later in this book doesn't mean you shouldn't start learning about them.

Develop a networking plan during law school and the initial years of practice. The law, as a service industry, is an industry of relationships. Those who run their own law firms need both to have comprehensive and varied contacts within the community, and they also need to start to develop a network of their own that is not dependent upon the firm they work for.

Networking. You'll hear this word thrown around. And you need to network. But how?

1. Get a Plan – Any Plan is Better Than No Plan

Chances are you are a perfectionist. It is a personality trait common in law students and lawyers. And law school makes this trait even worse. But writing a networking plan is more important than making the "perfect" one. You'll never have the perfect plan. Every project you make will get adjusted, tweaked, revised, and thrown away for a new plan. The key is to get a plan and start executing it.

2. Actionable Items: These are the things you can set out to do each day or week.

For instance, if you want to move to a new town, you might have an Actionable Item contacting at least one person on LinkedIn who lives there.

Set aside some time every day to make your plan come to life. It doesn't have to be much. Fifteen minutes a day will add up if you are consistent.

3. When: Make networking a priority. Priority plus consistency is a great asset.

4. Set reasonable expectations – you won't achieve all your goals immediately. But as you apply yourself to the

plan you have created, you will find that your consistent small effort turns into dividends.

As you network, viewing it as something that you will continue to do throughout your career is helpful. With that in mind, network with people you enjoy, go to events you like. Networking that is fun is something you will do.

CHAPTER TWO: THE BASICS

Where do you want to practice? Since opening a law firm is opening a business, it makes sense to figure out where you want to open your firm. Many large metros have too many lawyers. And many midsized to smaller communities have few lawyers, with many aging out of practice.

So consider where opening your firm will be most advantageous for your business.

- Small and midsize markets are wide open in many areas.
- Technology has made the practice of law much more uniform – no longer do you need a huge law library because you have all the research tools you need, and more, online.
- Look for areas that need lawyers and where the median age of lawyers is high – this is a zone of opportunity.
- Many smaller and mid sized markets have lower costs of living.

- Some types of law only exist in larger markets – so if this is your practice area reality, location matters.

Small legal markets have some definite pluses:

1. Usually, a lower cost of living.
2. A smaller Bar so more collegiality.
3. Less competition for jobs.
4. Often, you get to handle your own cases faster.
5. The potential to move up the ladder in a firm faster.
6. Greater community.
7. Better commute, if any.
8. The chance to be a part of the legal community and be known.
9. Lower office overhead.
10. Greater ability to dominate the market with SEO and other electronic advertising strategies.

Smaller markets also tend to have less billable requirements, and since the pace of life is often less hectic, you get to enjoy your work without having your work become your entire life.

The commute aspect of smaller markets is often fantastic. A 5- or 10-minute commute in a smaller market isn't uncommon.

Office Space:

The image of a lawyer with a large, ornate office looms large in television and the movies. And offices that are ornate and large are nice. But they are also expensive. As you start your law firm, look at your options for office space:

- Can you share space in a current law firm? And if you can, do you have the ability to get work they don't want and don't handle?
- What services are offered at the office space – copying, reception, parking, coffee, and water?
- Is the office space easy to find and easy to get to?
- Does the office space have more than one conference room? How do you reserve the conference room?
- Does the office come with a phone system? If so, do you have to use it? Is the phone system an added cost?
- Do you need to provide your own internet service, or can you use the one in the office location?
- Do you even need an actual office, or can you use a virtual office instead?

Office space is a cost. You should choose office space that allows you to minimize the recurring expense of rent, as overhead is something you want to ensure you control when starting a law firm.

It's also important to know your clientele. Do they have expectations about the type of office you have? Do they care? If your office is overly ornate, will they consider it a reason to think you are overcharging them?

On the practical side, office sharing makes much sense for someone just opening their law firm. It allows for more services at a lower price. And it means that you have other people to be around – being alone is often forgotten when people discuss opening their own firm. If you are the firm, until you grow, you are alone.

And, sometimes, you can office share with an older attorney or firm that is looking to find a successor.

Research Your Location:

It is well worth scouting your market and practice area before determining where to open your office. Before you open your office, get numbers on internet searches in your office area for your practice type. Determine how many lawyers are doing what you want to do in the area. Remember, for online ads, your office address is crucial, which will be discussed in more detail later.

What's In a Name:

Lawyers tend to name their firms using some variation of their name. In many states, this is no longer required under the rules. As people increasingly use non-referral sources to choose a lawyer, using your name as your firm's name may not be the wisest move. Instead, consider using a name that reflects what you do. As an example:

- Wills, Trust, and Estates Lawyers of Western Kansas is much better than The McCrea Law Firm.
- Family Lawyers of Bowling Green is much better than The Reginald Law Firm.
- Injury Lawyers of North Georgia is better than Booth, Hamilton, and Leonard.

In all of the examples above, assume that the law firms focus on the same practice areas in each instance. The names that include the practice area are much more to the point and leave no doubt in the customer's mind about what type of law the firm practices. Often lost in the name decision is that providing legal services is a business. So it would help if you had a name that allows people to easily understand what legal services you provide. Doing so gives you a competitive advantage. And it creates trust – you've named your firm after the services you provide, and this resonates with people.

Use Your Team:

As you consider the location of your firm and the name of your firm, you must coordinate this with your marketing provider. For instance, if you are using Cooper Saunders, you want to have a Zoom with him, go over locations and names, and get data. Data will help you decide where to locate your firm in your chosen geographic area and will help you name your firm.

- Business is a team spot.
- The law is a business and a profession.
- For the business aspects of the law, use your team.
- Leverage your team's knowledge and experience.
- Accept that you are not a business expert. It's ok.

Part of your future success is understanding that you need a team to grow, to expand, and to make your law firm successful. You cannot do it on your own.

Get Insurance:

It's not sexy, but you need malpractice insurance and likely premise insurance. Check around to see if your state bar has a good provider.

CHAPTER THREE: FIND YOUR "WHY"

B efore starting a law firm, every lawyer goes to law school. During those three years, you learn next to nothing about the private practice of law. And what you do learn centers around the profession of law rather than the business of law.

To some, describing the law as both a profession and a business is offensive. And this is a sentiment that abounds in law schools. But the law is a service profession, and services in a free market economy come at a price. You'd think that since most law firms are engaged in the private practice of law, the business of law would get discussed more. But it isn't.

And even worse, how to start your own law firm is rarely described or talked about, except in passing.

This book aims to solve a pressing issue in the law: It aims to help those who want to, who are planning, and even those who have started a law firm get a blueprint and a plan. It's 100% doable.

It's also essential to find your why. Why start a law firm? Why engage in the planning process now?

Everyone's "Why" varies. Find yours, and then let this book

help you engage in a systematic plan to make your "Why" a reality.

But before moving forward, you must discover your "Why." Please write it down. Think about it. This is the bottom level of the foundation of your law firm. Your "Why" will help guide you in making crucial decisions, from where to practice, who to hire, how many hours you want to work, how you want to bill, and how big you want your firm to become.

Included in your "Why," think about adopting an abundance mindset. The law is packed with people who have a scarcity mindset. The scarcity mindset fits well in a profession dealing with conflict, emotions, and catastrophes. But, if you throw out the scarcity mindset and adopt an abundance mindset, you will discover a new freedom. And with this new mindset, you will be prepared to implement the plans this book lays out.

CHAPTER FOUR: THE BUSINESS IS OUT THERE - HOW WILL PEOPLE FIND YOU?

For most people starting a law firm or wanting to start a law firm, the scariest aspect is finding business. Business comes to us in different ways. Let's talk about three common ways of getting business.

1. Networking for Business

As a law firm owner, you must get out in the community and inform people about your services. This is networking. Networking is a long-term business prospecting model. But just because it is a long-term model, don't avoid it. There are many reasons to network. And one often overlooked reason is that networking will help you to become a better salesperson. I can hear your protest now, "But I am not in sales; I am a lawyer." True, you are a lawyer. And you are a lawyer who is selling your service. So you are also in sales. Networking gives us plenty of chances to tell others what we do and how we can help, and it allows us to become a value-added part to those we know.

As for how to network, here's what I have learned - getting into a regular, consistent networking schedule with people who aren't lawyers will pay off. Add a stable, consistent networking schedule with lawyers, and you will have an excellent foundation of relationships in a few months to a year. From that foundation, you will find that consistency is your friend and that your "network" will grow faster and larger with less effort.

2. Referrals

Referrals are the product of your network. And while referrals are tied into networking, not all referrals will come from your network. Some will come from people who know your reputation. Others will come directly from your network.

Referrals are typically your best leads. They come with a built-in advantage - the person coming to see you already trusts you even though they don't know you. Why? Because they trust the person who referred them.

There is a temptation to view referral leads as "free." I'm afraid that's not right. They are not free. Instead, most referrals are the product of your networking and reputation building.

There is also a temptation to view a referral lead as a "sure thing." This is also wrong. Refrain from viewing a referral as certain business. Instead, consider a referral as someone who needs help, already has a good opinion of you, and, because of these two facts, someone to whom you can show your expertise and problem-solving skills without convincing them they need your services.

It's essential to keep a list of who is referring your business. The people who refer matters to you believe in you. They are not to be taken for granted. And you must have a system to ensure you handle referrals with the utmost care.

3. Marketing

The untapped gold mine for your new firm lies in effective marketing. A marketing genius writes the following chapters. I cannot add to them in any technical sense. But I can talk about what is often missing in many law firms that engage in online marketing.

You need to have an online marketing presence. And you need to figure out how to service the leads that come. This is missing in almost every law firm, and because it is missing, law firms are leaving money on the table and not taking full advantage of their marketing.

The goal of marketing, be it print, online, SEO, or Google ads, is to maximize your return on investment. The following took me years to fully grasp. And nobody is talking about it in law school. Let's break it down into simple terms.

1. You have a budget for marketing.
2. You want to determine how many leads your budget will bring you monthly.
3. You can only calculate reasonable leads if your marketer can show you like kind law firm data. So, you must ask for data and case studies. If you hire Cooper, it's easy. He has an abundance of both.
4. Next, you need to understand how long it will take to get you the leads. SEO takes longer to generate leads than Google ads, for example.
5. How much is each new case worth? Is a new case averaging to $3500.00?
6. Once you know the average case value and the average number of leads, you can start to determine how many cases you need to break even, how many you need to turn a modest profit, and how many you need to achieve a 7 or 10 times return on investment.

7. How will you service each incoming lead? Each lead is worth $ 3,500.00 in my example. How will you convert each incoming lead? Speed is of the essence - you absolutely must have a system in place to speak with your lead immediately or almost immediately.
8. Why? Why do you need to act with speed? Because you are a commodity. This lesson is lost on most lawyers. We're a gas station, plumber, or electrician we're a commodity.
9. So, you need to invest time to develop your system of servicing each lead immediately.

A long time ago, I wanted to start my firm. I had no clue how to do it. I leaped blindly into the world of law firm ownership. Along the way, I made many mistakes. And I needed a guide. But I didn't have one and didn't know where to get one. As you read the following chapters, pay close attention to what Cooper is teaching. I am 100% convinced that if you understand what he is trying to teach you, you will find more success than you dreamed of.

PART II

MARKETING A LAW FIRM

BY COOPER SAUNDERS

CHAPTER FIVE: FOUNDATION & EXPERT STATUS

"Cooper. No offense, but I have tried to grow my law firm with marketing but have never seen results. So, with all due respect, how are you different from every other marketing guru?"

In Jim Collins' best-selling book Good To Great, he explains the importance of finding and understanding your hedgehog concept.

"Are you a hedgehog, or a fox? The fox knows many things, but the hedgehog knows one big thing. The fox is a cunning creature, able to devise a myriad of complex strategies for sneak attacks upon the hedgehog. Day in and day out, the fox circles around the hedgehog's den, waiting for the perfect moment to pounce. Fast, sleek, beautiful, fleet of foot, and crafty—the fox looks like a sure winner. The hedgehog, on the other hand, is a dowdier creature, looking like a mix- up between a porcupine and a small armadillo. He waddles along, going about his simple day, searching for lunch and taking care of his home.

The fox waits in cunning silence at the juncture in the trail. The hedgehog, minding his own business, wanders right into the path of the fox. 'Aha, I've got you now' thinks the fox. He leaps out, bounding across the ground, lightning fast. The little hedgehog, sensing danger, looks up and thinks 'Here we go again. Will he ever learn?" Rolling up into a perfect little ball, the hedgehog becomes a sphere of sharp spikes, pointing outward in all directions. The fox, bounding toward his prey, sees the hedgehog defense and calls off the attack.

Retreating back to the forest, the fox begins to calculate a new line of attack. Each day, some version of this battle between the hedgehog and the fox takes place, and despite the greater cunning of the fox, the hedgehog always wins."

What is my hedgehog concept? When I work with law firms, I understand that generating more cases is my job. I focus on the tools that will generate the best results and stick with that.

Most companies these days are like the fox. They have plenty of tools and tactics, but they do not have one simple quality that they are best at. Unlike the hedgehog, that can fend off almost all attacks with one simple move.

That's why we don't offer year-long contracts. If we don't perform, my clients will leave, and I will go out of business. But I know I can get your law firm results, and when I do, you will want to stay. I want my clients to work with me because the return they receive is at least ten times what they invest.

In chapter nine, I describe what you need to look for when hiring a digital marketing company.

Why Marketing Fails

When marketing plans fail, it's usually because they need more **focus**. To make your plan work, choose a niche and focus on marketing avenues that bring cases to your law firm. In this book, I will guide you through the process. Remember, success leaves clues. Other law firms have experienced success with marketing, and I will show you how they did it.

RICHES ARE IN THE NICHES!

What is a niche? A niche is a subcategory of the law you are practicing. Let's say you are a personal injury lawyer; a niche would be motorcycle accidents or trucking accidents. Focusing on one of these niches would allow you to create an effective marketing strategy to produce results.

I will hit on this throughout the book, but your law firm can be a personal injury law firm that handles cases across the board. But, you should only market to a niche. And I know what you are already thinking: Why would I not market to every service we offer?

Here's why:

1. Unless you have a marketing budget the size of Coca-Cola, you will run out of money before generating any results.
2. Your marketing message will become diluted and weak.
3. Your brand relevance will suffer. You want people to see your law firm and advertisements and say, "Hey, that's for me!"

A 100-watt light bulb and a 100-watt laser have the same energy, but their uses and effects differ dramatically. The light bulb can brighten a room in a home, while the laser can cut through steel. The key difference is how the energy is focused. The same is true for your marketing efforts: the focus of your efforts can greatly impact the results you achieve.

Here is an example to illustrate this point. I met with a law firm in Dallas. Unfortunately, they fell into the trap most law firms do. They were a criminal defense law firm marketing every service it provided, thinking that if the law firm had a wide enough net, they would have a better chance of generating clients.

After completing the steps in this chapter, we focused all of our marketing efforts, such as Local SEO and Google Ads, on DUI cases. We confirmed there were enough searches to keep their law firm busy.

Once we broke free of their competition and achieved the goal of total market domination for DUI cases, a funny thing started to happen. The owner of the law firm called me and said, "Hey, Cooper! Suddenly, we are receiving an enormous amount of referrals for the other services we offer. Is this something you did? Did we start another campaign?"

Why did this law firm, which very rarely used to get referrals and repeat business, start getting them in abundance? Because they finally broke free from their competitors and were getting seen consistently. No longer were they one out of hundreds of law firms in

Dallas offering criminal defense services. They were the #1 law firm in Dallas for DUI cases. Big difference! And since they did an amazing job for the DUI defense, the customers only assume they will be amazing at the other services they provide. Without focus, this law firm wouldn't have met these clients in the first place.

This is the main essence of the entire marketing plan. Before we started working with this law firm, these were all the services they were marketing on Google Ads with a $2,500-a month budget split evenly for each service.

- Criminal Defense
- Traffic
- Assault

- Burglary
- Robbery
- Homicide
- DUI
- Sexual Assault
- Drug Crimes
- Domestic Violence
- White-collar crimes

What is the amount of money allocated to each service? $227. On top of that, the ads weren't created for each service, giving his ads a lower relevance score and making them more expensive. Bad combination!

Before he listed all of these services, he told me he had used a previous marketing company and hadn't received any results from them. Can you see why?

Instead, we allocated the entire $2,500 budget solely to DUIs and created the ads to speak directly to this service. His competitors didn't stand a chance!

While your competitors are wasting their dollars trying to be seen for every service, you will be the shining beacon of light that gets all the attention for the service you choose, not the leftovers. Eventually, down the road, we can expand. But for now, you need to choose your niche.

Before We Begin

Are you ready for one of the most important tips I can give you? You are in sales. I can generate your law firm calls and leads, but closing the leads is your job. Not only that, but you also need to ensure all your staff who deal with clients regularly have sales training. I had a personal injury client in Houston who was ranking for over 80 personal injury keywords. This is no small achievement. Our services were generating around 150 calls a month. When we had our monthly meeting, the client was not happy. He told us these leads were generating him no business, and he was concerned about the return on investment he was receiving from our services.

I was stunned. I went into that meeting thinking we would exchange high fives, but instead, it was a come to Jesus talk. I thought to myself, this can't be right. There are too many calls for all of them to be bad.

So, I decided to see what would happen if I called the office. First call? No answer. And to top it off, the voicemail was full. Second call? Nothing again. Finally, on the third call, someone answered, and you would have thought I called at 1 AM on Christmas morning. A loud "HELLO??" came through the phone, and I asked, "Is this the XYZ Law Firm?" After a moment of silence, she said, "Uh yeah? What do you want?"

I immediately hung up the phone and called my client. I asked him if he had ever mystery shopped his receptionist. He replied, "No. Why? She has been here since I started the firm."

I told him I found out why our calls weren't generating new business. After he did some testing himself, he got her into a sales course, and now his law firm has just doubled the previous year's revenue. What is the moral of the story? When you start your law firm, ensure you and your staff understand the importance of sales. If not, growing your law firm will be an uphill battle.

For the best information on this subject, pick up two books. They are written by Bryan Tracy—The Secrets Of Closing The Sale and The Psychology of Selling.

THE FOCUS MARKETING METHOD VISUAL

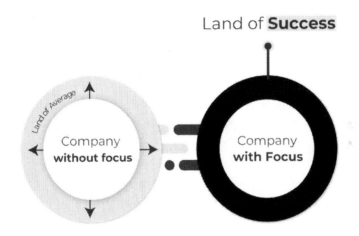

Land of **Success**

Land of Average

Company **without focus**

Company **with Focus**

How To Choose A Niche

Here is the process I take my clients through when we are looking to identify a niche. I always tell my clients, "The single most important thing to me is making sure your law firm is generating cases from my services." To ensure this happens, I must confirm that there are enough searches to make it worth our time. If not, the client won't generate enough business, and I will be headed out the door.

Luckily, Google offers a free tool called the Google Keyword Planner. This tool gives you data on the number of searches for a particular keyword in a month, the competition surrounding this keyword, and how much money people are bidding for this keyword.

You need to pay attention to the number of monthly searches for each keyword surrounding the niche. Would this keep you busy if you received 10% of the calls and inquiries from the monthly searches? (Even though our data shows our law firms see around 30-50%.) If the answer is yes, then you are ready to rock and roll. Open an Excel sheet and add ten to fifteen keywords you want to dominate. For example, if you want to be the number one semi-truck accident lawyer in Kansas City, your keyword list would look something like this:

- Semi truck accident attorney
- Semi truck accident attorney Kansas City
- Semi truck accident attorney near me
- Semi truck accident lawyer
- Semi truck accident lawyer near me
- Semi truck accident lawyer Kansas City
- Best semi truck accident attorney
- Best semi truck accident attorney near me
- Best semi truck accident attorney in Kansas City

And so on. Ensure you write down the average monthly searches next to each keyword.

Also, this tool will give you insight into which city or area you want to target. Let's say you are split between starting a law firm in Denver or a suburb such as Lakewood. You can use this tool to understand the differences in search volume and cost differences between the two cities; if you don't have to pick a fight with an 800-pound gorilla, don't.

If you want more information on choosing a niche and what process I take my clients through to identify a profitable niche, visit StartYourLawFirmToday.com/niche.

The Foundation

With your niche identified, it's time to build your foundation. Building a successful law firm is a lot like building a skyscraper. To do this, you must have a solid foundation. If not, your building won't get very far. If the foundation of your marketing plan is flawed, everything else you do will be for nothing.

Most law firms hire marketing companies, see terrible results, and don't understand why. Lawyers don't realize that it wasn't the building but the foundation that made the campaign a waste. They hire another marketing company, and their terrible experience happens again and again until they can no longer take it. Then, they either resign themselves to only focusing on referral business, or worse, they close their doors entirely. Let's discuss the foundation you need to create to ensure your law firm doesn't turn into the leaning tower of average.

The foundation of your law firm consists of the following building blocks:

- Branding
- Website Basics
- Expert Status
- Social Media

Each one of these steps is crucial for you to have implemented in your law firm if you want to see any success in marketing.

Branding

I have a pet peeve that I would like to share with you, although you may not be interested. It bothers me when people choose random business names, like "Monarch Law." While it may seem original and stylish, our main goal is to make money. If you name your business something vague like "Monarch Law," it will be difficult for potential customers to understand what you offer. Instead, I suggest naming your law firm something more descriptive, such as "The Monarch Estate Planning Law Firm." That way, customers can easily understand what services you provide.

I was speaking to a lawyer just starting his firm, and he stopped me and said, "But wait. What about companies such as Nike and other law firms in my area that are massive? It doesn't seem like they have a problem."

Sure! If you are fine with spending your hard-earned money so people can understand what your law firm provides, go for it. I would rather you spend your money getting in front of people looking to hire your law firm.

That's all for my rant.

To establish your brand in your niche, focus on excellent branding and messaging. For a new law firm, choose a name that reflects your niche, such as The KC Motorcycle Crash Lawyers or The Jane Doe Motorcycle Accident Lawyers.

Attached is an example of the branding of a law firm we created.

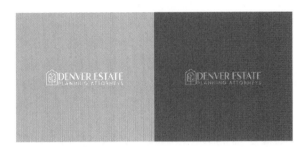

Here is the checklist of things you will need to complete your branding:

- Name that will rank well on Google and makes sense to your target market
- Domain (www.motorcyclecrashlawyerxyz.com)
- Website
- Logo
- Colors
- Font
- Social Media
- Google Business Profile
- Slogan

For your branding basics, such as your logo, colors, and font, head over to Fiverr.com. They have great brand creation services for around $60. But here's a fair warning: Do not buy link-building or SEO services. All this will do is load your website with toxic backlinks.

FIT THE PART WITH CONSUMER NEUROSCIENCE

When creating your law firm's brand identity, it's important to consider the subtle messages you may be communicating to potential clients on a subconscious level. Neuroscience studies how the brain impacts our decisions and actions.

As such, their insights can prove invaluable to marketers looking to create a brand that connects with clients on a deeper, more intuitive level. By tapping into the latest research on the brain and its workings, law firms can craft a brand identity that resonates with clients and communicates the right message about their values, expertise, and approach to legal services.

Referring to the book *How Psychology Works*, they state:

"Rather than relying on what consumers tell them—and many individuals either cannot or choose not to express their preferences—neuro marketers see how the brain activity of volunteers is stimulated by emotions, the key to deciding whether to buy something."

"Research has shown, for instance, that activity increases in the mesolimbic (reward-linked) brain area when participants are shown cars they find attractive and that people's decisions change when they are more hungry, stressed, or more tired than usual."

Now that you understand how important visuals are to your law firm's overall marketing and branding let's look at the specific examples in *How Psychology Works*.

Fonts - How appealing the letters look and how easy they are to read affect whether the consumer wants to read the message they contain. As a law firm, you want a font that shows you are the authority. Avoid scripts and fussy fonts with unnecessary flourishes.

Videos - Moving images can tell a story well and appeal to consumers who are used to getting their information from television and video clips on the Internet or social media. Have a video on your website explaining your process and how you are the expert for their case.

The Psychology of Color - Colors, above all, communicate mood and emotion and provoke a reaction. So designers and marketers choose a color to fuse the nonverbal spirit with the message the company or brand wants to convey.

- *Green*: Foliage and bright greens look restful and suggest a product is natural, healthy, restorative, reassuring, a new beginning, environmentally aware, and fresh. Darker, emerald green speaks to wealth. If your niche deals with money, I really love this dark green.
- *Red*: Bright red gets a fiery response: exciting, sexy, passionate, urgent, dramatic, dynamic, stimulating, adventurous, and motivating.
- *Blue*: Sky blue seems calm, dependable, serene, and suggestive of infinity, whereas bright blue crackles with energy. Dark blue has authority and is associated with professionals, uniforms, banks, and tradition. If your niche deals with people in a tight or stressful situation, blue is an amazing color to go with.

- *Pink*: While light pink comes across as innocent, delicate, romantic, and sweet sometimes verging on the sentimental - bright pink, like red, is a hot, sensual, attention-seeking, energetic, and celebratory color.
- *Purple*: Linked to intuition and imagination, purple is a contemplative, spiritual, and enigmatic color, especially on the bluer side. Red purples imply something more thrilling, creative, witty, and exciting.

Shapes - Geometric shapes make a product look dependable and familiar, whereas organic forms suit a creative idea. If you want your clients to see you as dependable and familiar, include geometric shapes in your branding.

Personalization - One of the most important and over-looked aspects of marketing is personalization. Have a professional photographer come in and take photos of you and your office. Take photos of you doing research and meeting with "clients." (They can be actors if none of your clients want to be photographed.) Show this potential client that you are a real person. They want to feel like they already know you once they make a call.

Isn't it incredible we can't even describe what we like on a conscious level? That is why it is so important to understand what humans actually want to see. That being said, visual responses are the best way we'll have a profound neurological impact on how humans make decisions without them even knowing it. In addition, having high-quality visuals draws customer attention and increases their engagement. This ensures more people use your law firm.

Website

What are the main roles your website plays in your law firm?

- To convert visitors into leads and ultimately into customers
- Rank high on search engines

There is a cold war between my website designers and my SEO team for this very reason. It doesn't matter how amazing the website is. The website is useless if no one can find it, and it doesn't convert traffic into leads. (Can you tell whose side I am on?)

Your website should be built to be a lethal sales tool for your law firm. Guide the visitor along a path that ultimately leads them to contact your law firm. And please, please, ensure your website is built with WordPress.

When people visit your website for the first time, especially in the first four seconds, spell out exactly how you can help them and an easy way to contact you. Remember, if you confuse them, you lose them.

If you are a motorcycle injury law firm, the first thing visitors should see is **Motorcycle Injury Lawyers in [City]**!

One of the most powerful ways to stand out from the crowd is to create a video outlining who you are and the process you take to ensure you obtain the best results for your clients. If possible, slip some testimonials from past clients in there for some social proof. Then, talk about your niche and why you are the best law firm to handle their unique case.

About Us

The "About Us" page is the second most visited page on law firm's websites after the home page. What does that say about your potential customer's buying habits? They want to know more about you and connect on a personal level. When they get in touch with your law firm, they want to feel as if they already know you.

So, let's walk through how to set up an about us page that turns visitors into leads. I have tested this outline over many years, and the following format has generated the best results for my clients.

Step One: Your Story

The first thing you need to outline is your story. What does your law firm believe in? Why did you start this law firm? What are your values and overall mission? Why do you get up every morning? What drives you? Explain why you chose your niche.

Step Two: The Characters

Who is behind the law firm? Have professional headshots and links to each team member's bio pages and LinkedIn accounts. Consumers no longer want to work with faceless corporations; they want to work with real people. So show off your personality and let them connect with you and your law firm.

Step Three: The Conflict

Why did you start this law firm or focus on this specific niche? What did you see in the marketplace that didn't sit right with you? Did you work for a big law firm and notice they really didn't care about their clients? I started WiseGuys Digital Marketing because another company took advantage of my grandparents. What is your story?

Step Four: The Resolution

What problem did you solve? And how did you solve this problem? Did allocating your resources to become the best at this niche help? Show proof that this resolution is effective and that you can solve their needs. Include awards, testimonials, etc.

Step Five: The Dialogue

What does your law firm sound like? Do you use specific jargon and lingo? People who ride motorcycles communicate differently than skateboarders. This is where you will insert the "About Us" video.

Step Six: The Call To Action

How can they get in touch with your law firm? Make this easy; only give them one choice. Should they call? Should they fill out a form submission? If you confuse them, you lose them! One of the best ways to use client testimonials is to place them under the call to action. You want as much firepower as possible when asking someone to commit.

Step Seven: The Setting

Where is your law firm located? Add photos of your building and the inside of your office. Show your awards and anything else you want your potential clients to see.

Always remember, when people visit the About Us page,

they are trying to get to know who you are on a personal level. So open up a bit and connect with them. Drop the facade and show them you are a real person just trying to help.

We aren't going to hit on how to optimize your website to rank on search engines just yet; we will cover that in the coming chapters.

Creating A USP

What is going to set you apart from your competition? What does your law firm offer that your competitors don't? Everyone in business is trying to answer the age-old question,

"What will get customers to choose my business over my competition?"

Last year, I was hired to perform market research for a law firm desperately trying to understand what would make them stand out from their competitors.

Problems and frustrations are the most valuable thing when operating a business. Problems create industries and inspire innovations that solve problems and improve lives. Simply put, Problems = Money. Pinpointing these problems can be difficult, but not anymore.

"All failed companies are the same. They were unable to escape competition" - Peter Theil.

The One-Star Improvement Plan

To start, you first need to hop on Google and search for the law firms that operate in the same niche as you do. Look at the onestar reviews from your competitors and across the nation. Create a document and gather around one hundred one-star reviews.

Once you have the reviews before you, identify four or five that arise more often than the rest. Once you have these, you need to see which frustration you can solve. For example, here were the top five we found for the law firm we performed this market research for:

- Poor communication about case details
- Rude/Dismissive
- Too busy to care about the client
- Complaint about a case/Specific lawyer
- Unhappy with the result

As you can see, you cannot solve the last two complaints. But look at the first three.

Could you solve these issues?

When I implemented this technique for WiseGuys, I noticed three complaints that stood out.

- Year-long contracts
- Lack of transparency
- Poor results

We eliminated year-long contracts, prioritized transparency, and focused on being the best at what we do. This gave us an edge over our competitors. Once you identify and resolve these issues, you can use them as selling points to win new customers.

Be Seen As The Expert

Being seen as the expert in your niche by your target market is critical as a lawyer. In many situations, contacting a lawyer about an issue or problem is the most important thing to happen in a person's life. Step into their shoes. They want to know the law firm representing them knows what they are doing and is the expert. Another perk is that you can charge more than your competitors and get the best cases.

So, how do you show you are an expert in your field? Create content. You can create content in many ways, such as blogs, podcasts, and cheat sheets, but I will cover my favorite method of generating content for law firms. The key to successful content creation is leverage. Create once and use it for a long time.

Creating Webinars

Webinars are the best way to paint yourself as an expert in your field. For example, a webinar topic could be "The 5 Things You Need To Do If You Get A DUI In [City] In [Year]!"

As you noticed, I included the year in there. This is because people want to know if the content is relevant. Nothing is more frustrating than clicking a YouTube video or reading an article made in 2013. But the more important aspect is you can duplicate the same piece of content every year and change a couple of things if the laws change.

Once your webinar is completed, you can hire a virtual assistant on Upwork to edit this content and use it in a range of places, such as:

- Upload it to YouTube
- Chop up the videos and post them on social media
- Take the audio from the webinar and post it as a podcast
- Transcribe the webinar and publish it as a blog post
- Create a downloadable cheatsheet to accompany this webinar to generate leads

Once you do a webinar on "The 5 Things You Need To Do If You Get A DUI In [City] In [Year]!" That might be a 15-20 minute piece of content. You want to ensure you are covering the topic in detail. But, within that piece of content, there are bullets that you can grab and use for social media content. These pieces of content might only be a couple of minutes long. You can cut these up and post them on your social media, website, and YouTube. The client base will think to themselves, "Wow! This law firm is providing value to my life, and if they are making content like this, they must know what they are talking about!"

If you don't like being on camera, you can create the webinar with your camera off and do a screen recording, even though it isn't as powerful. People want to see and connect with you. Some of the most successful webinars I have witnessed my clients make looked unprofessional, but the content was phenomenal. People want authenticity and value! Use this to your advantage!

That brings us to the next topic, which is often misunderstood by lawyers: how to utilize social media.

Social Media

If utilized correctly, social media can generate a lot of business for your law firm. But, most lawyers have yet to learn how to approach it. So, let's start by understanding the bird's eye view of social media.

Social media is how you show people you are the expert. Creating webinars and educational content does no good if no one sees it.

Social media is a place where people go to escape from reality. They want to hop on Facebook or Instagram and see what their friends are doing. The best way to think of social media is a social gathering. Would you ever walk around a party, handing out business cards, trying to pitch people to use your service? Would anyone want to talk to you? Never!

But what if you were talking about something that came up at work, letting everyone know what you do in an indirect way that is entertaining? This is how you need to approach social media. First, you need to capture the attention and interest of your audience without directly pitching them. Then, when they do need your services, they will remember you and give you a call. Give out information that will interest your target audience, post testimonials from previous cases, and updates on the current landscape.

This is where the repurposing of your content will become your best friend. Since it is in video format, people will watch it. People hate reading these days, especially on social media. So now, when creating your webinar, keep this in the back of your mind. Can you throw in interesting stories or case studies that would benefit your social media presence?

Your main goal is to entertain and generate engagement. That is why influencers always say, "Like if you agree" or "Comment if you disagree." All they want is the interactions.

Show off your knowledge and build a loyal following.

You can use the same content for your personal page as well as your law firm page.

Use tools such as Hootsuite to schedule posts months in advance and post them to all your social media accounts simultaneously. Depending on your chosen niche, you should be more active on the social media platform your target market hangs out on.

Social media isn't the most important thing to focus on as a lawyer, but it can help cement your expert status for your niche.

Chapter Summary

You will be ready to conquer the world once you identify your niche and set up your online foundation. The four foundational pieces are:

1. Branding
2. Website Basics
3. Expert Status
4. Social media

After you have completed this step in the process, it is time to learn how to get your law firm in front of ready-to-buy prospects.

CHAPTER SIX: SEO

So, now we have a niche identified for your law firm, it is time to understand the best ways to generate cases, starting with Local SEO. The first step in generating cases for your firm is to get in front of people who are already looking for solutions to their problems.

Over Labor Day weekend, I was visiting my buddy's lake house. We took turns jumping off the top of his dock and catching a football. Of course, it got very competitive, and I went for a ball that was a bit out of my reach. My ear took most of the impact when I landed, and I was in pain. I hopped in my car and found the nearest store selling Advil. Do you think I looked at the price? No. Did the clerk have to convince me to buy it? No. I was in pain, and I wanted it solved right away. What is the best way to sell Advil? Get in front of people with a blistering headache. The same goes for marketing your law firm.

Let's start by understanding Local SEO and the importance of this tool in growing your law firm.

Local SEO is not the fastest way to generate clients, but it will generate the best cases for the least amount of money for your law firm. In the next chapter, we will discuss how to get the phone ringing for your law firm almost instantly with Google Ads. But first, we must understand the Local Map Pack and why it was created.

THE LOCAL MAP PACK

"The 'Google Map Pack' (or the Google Local Map Pack) is a prominent section in the Google local search results that showcases the top-ranking local listings for your location or the search location.

In the Google Map Pack, businesses are listed alongside

their geographic location, contact information, hours, and other helpful information.

Users can click on a listing to learn more about the company, call the contact number, or pull up Google Maps navigation to the business's physical location." -Searchenginejournal.com

So why does the Local Map Pack matter for your law firm? Google Maps aims to make it easier for users to find and interact with the business or law firm they are looking for in a local search, especially on their mobile devices.

The best return on investment is when law firms rank #1 in the Local Map Pack for their Core Service. This is the Holy Grail for law firms. Let's look at what you can expect with Local SEO regarding ROI.

Let's break down the numbers of a law firm that ranks #1 in its marketplace for personal injury cases. This is a client, but I have decided to hide their identity. When I meet with a potential client, I always pull out a case study from a previous client who chose the same niche in the same size market.

This allows me to give you an accurate estimate of how many calls I can generate for your law firm. Current clients have told me this is their favorite part of the process. They are used to going into marketing plans without really knowing what type of results to expect. With me, you will get an inside look at what the marketing plan will generate in terms of calls and leads.

Rankings Table

Keyword	Google		Google Mobile		Google Maps		Bing		Bing Local	
	Rank	Change	Rank	Change	Rank	Change	Rank	Change	Rank	Change
truck accident attorney	●	●	Loc	●	●	Loc	1	●	-	-	-	-
	-	-	Org	-	-	Org						
truck accident lawyer	●	●	Loc	●	●	Loc	1	●	-	-	-	-
	-	-	Org	-	-	Org						
semi truck accident lawyer	-	-	Org	-	-	Org	1	●	-	-	-	-
	●	↑	Loc	●	↑	Loc						
Brain Injury Law Firm	●	●	Loc	●	●	Loc	1	●	-	-	-	-
car accident lawyer near me	●	●	Loc	●	●	Loc	1	●	-	-	-	-
car crash lawyer	●	●	Loc	●	●	Loc	1	●	●	●	Loc	1	●
injury lawyer	●	●	Loc	●	●	Loc	1	↑ 1	●	●	Loc	2	●
	-	-	Org									
slip and fall lawyer	●	●	Loc	●	●	Loc	1	●	-	-	-	-
class action lawyer near me	●	↑ 1	Loc	4	●	Org	1	↑ 1	-	-	-	-
	4	●	Org	●	↑ 1	Loc						
class action attorney near me	●	●	Loc	●	●	Loc	1	●	-	-	-	-
	5	↑ 2	Org	5	↑ 2	Org						
medical malpractice attorney	●	●	Loc	●	●	Loc	1	●	-	-	-	-
	19	↑ 2	Org	19	↑ 5	Org						
Motorcycle Accident Injury Lawyer	●	●	Loc	●	●	Loc	1	●	-	-	-	-
	21	↑ 4	Org	20	↑ 4	Org						
medical malpractice lawyer	●	●	Loc	●	●	Loc	1	●	-	-	-	-
	24	↑ 15	Org	22	↑ 14	Org						
▮▮▮▮ injury attorney	●	●	Loc	●	●	Loc	1	●	7	↑ 1	Org	18	↑
	29	↑ 4	Org	30	↑ 4	Org			33	↑ 1	Org	
best personal injury lawyer	●	●	Loc	●	●	Loc	1	●	●	●	Loc	1	●
	37	↑ 1	Org	35	↑ 1	Org						
accident injury lawyer near me	●	●	Loc	●	●	Loc	1	●	●	●	Loc	1	●
	38	↑ 1	Org	13	↑	Loc						
Personal injury lawyer near me	●	●	Loc	●	●	Loc	1	●	●	●	Loc	1	●
	38	↑ 5	Org	35	↑ 1	Org						
injury attorney	●	●	Loc	●	●	Loc	1	●	●	●	Loc	2	↑ 1

Again, if you would like the entire case study, schedule a time to chat with me at wiseguysdm.com/contact.

This law firm chose "Semi Truck Accidents" as its first niche. Notice our plan didn't start with ranking for all of these services. We chose "Semi Truck Accidents" and expanded from there. If we had begun with all these keywords, there is no doubt we would still be working toward ranking number 1 for any of these keywords. Now, they rank number 1 for all Personal

Injury Keywords in their marketplace. The red 'A' means they rank #1 in the Local Map Pack for the keyword.

- Average Monthly Searches: 450
- Average Monthly Calls and Form Submissions: 66
- Average Monthly Conversion Rate: 34-52%

I am a big fan of Local SEO because it allows law firms of any size to rank number one in search results. If you were to use PPC to reach the same level of visibility, it would cost you anywhere between $60,000 to $120,000 per month, depending on the market size. This law firm generates a monthly caseload ranging from $50,000 to $50,000,000, an incredible return on investment. They get to choose the cases they work on and only accept the ones best suited for their practice.

If you want a case study from your niche and location, contact me at Wiseguysdm.com/contact.

Now that you know the return you can generate from Local SEO, let's understand how you can rank your law firm #1 in the Local Map Pack.

Local SEO

As I mentioned, Local SEO and ranking #1 in the Local Map Pack is the Holy Grail for bringing consistent cases. An entire book could be written on this subject alone, so I will outline the most important aspects Google looks at when ranking a local business.

At the end of the day, Google wants the best user experience for the people who search on their platform. They want to ensure the businesses at the top of their rankings stay active and have a solid reputation. So, let's jump into how to rank your law firm #1 in the Local Map Pack.

Create Or Claim Google Business Listing

To start, you need to claim or create a Google Business Listing. Without your business listing, your law firm will not rank in the Local Map Pack. The best way to check for this is to go to Google and search for your law firm. There will be text that says, "Own This Business?" Click on this and ensure it has been claimed. If it has not, go through the steps to confirm your listing.

If your law firm doesn't show up, you must create a new listing. Open Google, and type https://www.google.com/business/. Once here, click "Manage Now," then, in the top right corner, there will be an "Add Business" button. Enter your law firm's information. They will likely have you verify by calling or sending you a postcard.

OPTIMIZE GOOGLE BUSINESS PROFILE

For simplicity's sake, I will go through each step you need to take to optimize your Google Business Profile from the top down.

Assess Your Competition

One of the first things I do when I meet with a potential client is to assess their current competition. So open up Google, search for your niche, and see what law firms come up in the Local Map Pack.

- How many reviews do they have? Have they replied to them?
- What does their cover photo look like?
- How many photos do they have?
- What does their website look like?

- How often do they post updates?
- What are their updates about?

Business Name

Your business name must reflect your actual business name. For example, if you are the XYZ Law Firm, and your Google Business Profile says, "Motorcycle Injury Law," you could get suspended. That is why, in the previous chapter, I suggested creating a business name that ranks well on Google right out of the gate. So, if Google suspends your profile, you have the legal documents needed to submit to get your profile reinstated. Even something as simple as XYZ Law Firm 'Kansas City' could be suspended.

Business Category

Your law firm's primary category is the most important, and you must choose properly. The categories you choose will contribute to Google's determination of which searches to display your business for and determine which Google Business Profile features (like attributes, bookings, etc.) are available for you to use. There are thousands of categories to choose from.

Let's say you chose "Motorcycle Accident Lawyer" as your niche. Unfortunately, there will not be a category for this. So, you will need to select "Personal Injury Lawyer." But, if your business name is "Motorcycle Accident Lawyers," you will almost automatically rank in the top three for motorcycle cases.

Business Description

In the business description, outline the aspects of your law firm that make you unique.

Throw in some of the keywords and locations you want to rank for. Such as "Social Security Attorney Las Vegas." Try to fill in the 750 characters with rich content about your law firm.

Contact Information

A huge step in optimizing your Google Business Profile is ensuring your law firm's contact information is correct.

- Phone Number
- Website URL

Location and Areas

Your business address has to be a physical address. PO boxes or UPS boxes will not be accepted. If you work out of your home or want to rank in a city where your office isn't currently based, use coworking spaces instead of getting a PO box or UPS box. Most coworking spaces have mailboxes that serve as "Virtual Offices." The best part is they only cost around $50 a month.

Hours and More

Ensure the hours displayed on your Google listing correspond with those on your website. Once you confirm the hours match, go through the holidays and mark the days you will not be open.

Photos

This is one of the most important parts of your Google Business Profile. The photos on your business listing are the first impression potential customers will get of your law firm.

The first thing to do is upload a cover photo. This will be the first photo potential customers will see. I suggest you make the cover photo a picture of yourself or your law firm. Next, add your business logo. Please ensure the logo is properly sized. If not, it looks very unprofessional. Contact whoever made your logo and tell them, "I need this logo 500 x 500."

Add Updates

This form of microblogging enables businesses to post short pieces of content like Facebook. So, how often should you post? Once a week is the sweet spot we have found to work best to increase the rankings of the law firms we work with. But, again, consistency is key. Use snippets from the webinars you create.

Reviews

The reviews you generate on your Google Business Profile are one of the most important things you can do to ensure success. I know reviews are kind of a taboo subject for lawyers, but they are so important for rankings and building trust with your potential clients. We have become a review-based society. Studies have shown that we trust reviews from strangers more than personal recommendations from people we know and trust. Not only that, the more reviews you have, the higher you will rank in the Local Map Pack.

So, what is the easiest way to generate reviews for your law firm? To start, your business profile has a spot next to the reviews that says, "Get More Reviews." This will generate a link to take your client's right to the review form. When they are sitting in your office, preferably after you give them good news, ask them if they will leave you a review. Tell them it will only take 20 seconds and would mean a lot to you. Text them the link while they are sitting there. People are busy, and once they leave your office, it will be ten times as hard getting them to leave you a review.

Also, try to generate reviews consistently. When you read this section, you will want to blast this link to everyone who has ever used your law firm, generate a bunch of reviews, and never think about it again. Google wants to see reviews come in at a consistent rate.

Clients often are confused about why I am so intense about them generating reviews. Depending on your niche, these reviews could generate millions of dollars for your law firm over the lifetime of your firm. Since you are just getting started, ask your friends and family.

Also, if you notice that Google is not posting all the reviews you are generating, contact me at WiseGuysDM.com/Contact, and I will reinstate them for you.

Services

After this, you will head over to the services tab. This is where you will create the service and description for your niche. Then, fill in the service description with rich, helpful content. Few businesses, especially law firms, take the time to fill out the service description, so ensure you are doing this.

Q & A

The Q & A function is built to serve as a frequently asked question section. You can post your own questions and answer them. Q&As with the most thumbs up appear on the Google business profile. The "Ask a Question" button facilitates queries, and the "See all questions" link takes you to an overlay popup showing all queries. This is becoming an important new hub of social interactivity, customer support, and maybe a ranking factor. Just ensure you keep an eye out for spam and abuse.

Embed Google Maps In The Footer Of Your Website

Once you have created and optimized your Google Business Listing, you want to embed your business listing into the footer of your website, making it easier for users to find your law firm. This also helps Google connect the dots between your listing and your website.

Wrapping Up Google Business Profile

As I said above, Google wants to recommend active and reputable businesses. Google loves consistency. Ensure the information on your Google Business Profile aligns with the information about your law firm across the web.

Now that we have covered the most important aspect of ranking locally, there are a handful of other things Google looks at when ranking a local company. Below are the six other ranking factors Google uses to rank companies in the Local Map Pack.

- Reviews – (17%)
- On-page optimization – (16%)
- Links – (13%)
- Behavioral – (7%)
- NAP Citations – (7%)
- Personalization – (4%)

The First Ranking Factor: Google Business Profile

Ensure you spend most of your time optimizing your business listing before moving on to these other steps!

The Second Ranking Factor: Reviews

Reviews are not only important for ranking, but they are also a leading factor in driving traffic into paying customers. This includes your Google Business Profile and third-party ranking sites such as Yelp, BBB.org, and Bing Local, to name a few.

The Third Ranking Factor: On-page Signals

Individual on-page optimization factors include NAP data, keywords in the title, and domain authority. Each page of your website should follow the outline below. This will help Google understand the content on your website and what keywords you are looking to rank for.

Here's an example of what the structure of what your website page should look like:

-H1: Motorcycle Lawyers In Dallas
-H2: Why Choose XYZ Motorcycle Law Firm

    a. H3: Expert Law Firm
    b. H3: 24 Years of Experience
    c. H3: Over 200 Cases

-H2: How To Choose A Motorcycle Lawyer In Dallas

    a. H3: Look at our reviews
    b. H3: Understand our history

c. H3: Look at our previous cases

On-page signals are massively important for both traditional and Local SEO. Your website must have a page for each service you offer, and new content must be consistently added. To really grow in the location you want to rank for, you'll need to include the city or town in multiple places across your website. On top of this, you will need to use location-specific keywords in your metadata for titles and descriptions across your website.

TOPICAL AUTHORITY

Being seen as a topical authority by Google is crucial when ranking your law firm on search engines. Topical authority is earned by creating quality content on a specific niche or topic. Producing high-quality and informative articles can lead to more people trusting your website as an authoritative resource on a specific subject matter.

Your website needs to be seen by Google as a topical authority for your identified niche.

You must create content covering your subject in great detail to do this. Start by creating around fifty pages surrounding your topic. This will give you a massive advantage over your competitors.

The Fourth Ranking Factor: Link Signals

Link signals are the number of websites that link back to your website. I am sure you have heard the term "backlinks" before. This task won't be worth your time if you handle your Local SEO yourself. However, if you have a company handling your marketing, such as WiseGuys, we can get this done for you.

The Fifth Ranking Factor: Behavior Signals

Some examples of Behavior Signals include click-through rate, mobile clicks to call, and dwell time.

But in terms of importance in ranking in the Local Map Pack, Behavior Signals have steadily declined for three years. So, instead of focusing on how to influence user behavior, your time will be better spent generating reviews and optimizing your Google Business Profile.

The Sixth Ranking Factor: Citation Signals

Individual citation ranking factors include location data, IYP/aggregator NAP consistency, and citation volume. Having your Name, Address, and Phone Number data consistent across business directories such as Yelp, BBB.org, and Bing Local will be seen as more trustworthy and authoritative by Google.

This will also be an easy way to generate backlinks to your business website.

The Seventh Ranking Factor: Personalization Signals

Individual personalization ranking factors include search history, search location, and the device they are searching from. Therefore, if you search for your business, click on the Google Business Profile, and look at the website every day, you will always come up #1 when you search.

Always remember that Google is notorious for changing the qualities they look for when ranking businesses.

The nice thing about hiring a company like WiseGuys Digital Marketing is that we rank #1 in Kansas City for Digital Marketing, Marketing Agency, and Marketing. So, if we can beat out all companies claiming they are Local SEO experts, we can do it for you.

Local SEO is great, but it takes time to achieve the desired results. The next step will teach you how to generate quality leads for your niche in about two weeks. If you are ready to start generating results as soon as possible, let's move on to the next step.

CHAPTER SEVEN: GOOGLE ADS

Google ads are a money-printing machine if implemented correctly. Unfortunately, most law firms don't see Google ads this way. To illustrate this point, I recently met with a lawyer in Miami. When he called me, you could tell he was upset.

"Hey, Cooper. I got your number from a current client of yours. Do you have a moment to talk?" He continued, "I have a family law practice here in Miami, and I am worried about my marketing plan. I am spending a lot of money on Google ads, and it hasn't generated one single case!"

I replied, "Don't worry. I have heard this at least five times this week. I'll get you fixed up.

What is your monthly budget?"

"$5,500 a month. I mean, we are getting calls, but nothing of value! My marketing company just keeps telling me I need to spend more, but considering I haven't generated one case, I didn't think that was the problem."

Common Myth: To see results from Google ads, you must spend more than everyone else.

I asked, "Could you add me to your Google Ads account or send me the reports you are getting from your marketing company. Usually, I can tell what the problem is within 30 seconds of getting into your account."

Once he added me to his account, I immediately spotted several problems.

"Okay. I have good and bad news. Which do you want first?" I asked.

"Bad." he replied.

"Your Google ads are a mess. The good news is that I can fix them and bring cases to you in as little as a week." (Which I cover throughout this chapter.)

With a big sigh of relief, he replied, "When can you start?"

In this chapter, I will show you how to set up your Google ads for your law firm so this doesn't happen to you. Especially when you are just starting your law firm, you don't have the luxury of wasting money. By following the strategies, you can effectively use Google search ads to drive results for your law firm. Google's default settings are built for you to spend the most money. If you follow Google's suggestions, your budget will be gone before you know it.

When I implement Google ads for my clients, I always aim to generate at least $10 for every $1 spent. This is a good goal to strive toward.

While SEO and ranking organically in the Local Map Pack is the ultimate goal, this takes time. With Google ads, you can get the ads up and running in less than a week.

So, with that being said, let's go through how to set up your Google ads campaign. If you are a visual learner, I have created a free Google ads MasterClass you can watch at WiseGuysdm.com/GoogleAds.

QUALITY SCORE

Before you jump into creating your Google ads campaign, we need to understand Google's Quality Score and why it's important if you want the best return on your investment.

Remember, Google is a massive referral service. People come to Google looking for referrals when they need to find services or information. They ask their questions by typing them into the search bar, and Google provides results that answer them.

If you searched for mountain bikes and then Google returned results for dirt bikes, you aren't going to be happy. In the future, you may even use another search engine, such as Yahoo or Bing. This is why it's super important for Google to ensure the results it returns to users are relevant. This applies to both the paid search results and the organic search results.

In a basic form, quality score is Google's way of ensuring customers have the same high-quality referral experience from paid and organic search results. To ensure this, Google created the Quality Score.

There are four main components of your quality score:

1. Click Through Rate
2. Keyword/Ad Relevance
3. Keyword/Query Relevance
4. Landing Page Quality

Let's break each of these down in a little more detail.

Click-Through Rate (CTR)

Click-through rate or CTR is the percentage of people who click on your advertisement. The CTR is calculated by your clicks divided by your impressions times 100. So, if your advertisement is shown ten times, and out of those ten times, it generates one click, you would have a CTR of 10%. In other words, 10% of people who saw your advertisement clicked. The higher your CTR, the higher your quality score will be. If more people click your ads, it's a good signal to Google that your ad must be relevant.

But how does Google know what a good CTR is? They will compare your campaign to others bidding on the same keywords. Google has a ton of data from past advertisers and uses this information to determine if your CTR is good or bad.

Keyword/Ad Relevance

Relevancy between the keyword you are targeting and the text in your advertisement is super important. This means your advertisement's text must be relevant to the keyword(s) you are bidding on. This is why I preach the importance of focus in your marketing campaigns.

Keyword/Query Relevance

A user types the sentence phrase or question into the Google search box called a query. For example, if I search "Should I hire a divorce lawyer?" and you are bidding on this query, the ad that appears needs to be relevant to my search. As discussed above, Google understands that the more relevant a searcher's query is to an advertiser keyword and ad text, the more relevant and useful that overall user experience will likely be.

Landing Page Quality

Landing page relevance is the least weighted factor in determining your quality score, but it plays a vital role in converting traffic into leads. Again, everything must match from the top down, from your keywords to the ads and the landing page.

If someone clicks on your motorcycle accident lawyer advertisement and lands on a generic "Contact Us" page, your landing page quality score will suffer. Not only that, but the user won't be happy, and Google will be aware of this.

Why am I telling you all of this? Because your quality score depends on how much you pay per click. The lower your quality score, the more you will have to pay to get in front of people searching for your services. I've met with law firms that were spending a small fortune just to get outperformed by a law firm with half the budget. Don't let this be you!

CREATING YOUR GOOGLE ADS CAMPAIGN

Step #1: Google Ads Account

The first thing you need to do is ensure you have a Google ads account. These are free to make. Just search "Google ads" in the search bar, and it will bring you right to it.

Step #2: New Campaign

Once you are in your Google ads account, there will be a blue button that says "New campaign."

Step #3: Leads

Once you click this, it will bring you to a page to select the objective of your campaign. Choose "leads."

Step #4: Search

After you choose leads, you will want to create a "Search" campaign. In the next chapter, I will discuss how to generate results from YouTube and Display ads.

Step #5: Goal

Select the way you want to reach your goal. Choose "Form Submissions" or "Phone Calls." This is how your leads will get in touch with you! When you click "Form Submissions," Google will create a conversion action. You will need this when we discuss conversion tracking. Lastly, name your campaign to keep everything organized.

Step #6: Bidding

The next screen Google will take you to is the Bidding section. Let's take a deeper look at another vital aspect of Google ads. Now, in its most basic form, bidding strategies are how you will bid on your keywords. There are many different strategies to choose from, but I will outline what works best for your law firm.

There are three main bidding strategies. First, there are automated bidding strategies where Google will basically do everything for you. Semi-automated, which is where you have a lot of control, but you let Google's algorithm do some work for you. And then, there is a manual bidding strategy where you have complete control over your campaign.

The main bidding strategy I implement is Cost Per Acquisition (CPA). Before using this strategy, ensure your conversion tracking is in place. With this bidding strategy, Google works to maximize the number of conversions while still hitting your CPA. You set your CPA dollar amount at the campaign or ad group level. Then, Google decides when to show your ads, who to show them to, and how much to charge for each click so you reach your goal.

Let's say you know the average profit you generate for the Core Service you are promoting is, for example, $900. You could set the CPA at $200. The number would grow from there for more valuable cases.

Step #7: Search Network

After you choose your bidding strategy, the next step is the campaign settings. You can utilize two networks: the Search Network and the Display Network. For now, just choose The Search Network.

Choose the location you want to target. You should already know what city or area you want to dominate.

Step #8: More Settings

The next step is to choose the "More Settings" tab. This will give you additional options for your Google ads campaign. The one thing I want you to focus on is the "Ad Schedule." If your campaign aims to generate phone calls, only run ads when someone is available to take the calls. I've witnessed thousands of dollars get wasted simply because the ads generated calls while the office was closed. If your goal is to generate form submissions, you don't have to worry about this as much.

Step #9: Keywords & Ads

Now, it is time for the "Keywords and ads" section. Edit the "Ad group 1" to the niche you are promoting.

To start, let's discuss your keywords. Keywords are the

lifeblood of your Google ads campaign. If you bid on the wrong keywords or have too many, your ads will not perform well.

You will first open an Excel sheet and name it the [Niche] Campaign.

After this, you will head to the Google Keyword Planner and click "Discover new keywords." Next, type in your Core Service and choose the area you want to dominate.

Then click "Get results."

Once it is finished loading, grab all the keywords corresponding to the niche this campaign is promoting and paste them into your Excel sheet. When you have around 30-40 keywords surrounding your niche, you want to add Match Types to your keywords. If you ignore this step, as most people do, you'll burn through your budget in hours. On top of that, your conversion rates will be pitiful.

There are three match types:

- Broad match
- Exact match
- Phrase match

Let's break down each to understand which is best for your law firm.

Broad Match

If you don't tell Google how and when to show your keywords, it will default to this setting and show your ads for any search it considers relevant. This could include searches that use your keywords in any order or don't even contain your keywords at all.

So if your keyword is:

- DUI Lawyer

With no punctuation or brackets, Google could show your ads for searches, such as:

- Law firm near me
- Do I need a lawyer?
- Estate planning lawyer
- Become a lawyer

This was one of the problems the lawyer faced at the beginning of the chapter. He was getting calls, but from keywords he didn't know he was bidding on! If you have run Google ads and generated leads and calls from random cases, this is why. Having the incorrect match type is where most law firms lose a tremendous amount of money.

Exact Match

This option gives you total control. You no longer have to worry about spending your marketing dollars on keywords that aren't relevant to your campaign. This step alone will save you thousands of dollars in wasted marketing assets. To use the Exact Match option, throw brackets around your keyword.

So if your keyword is:

- Motorcycle Crash Lawyer

Your law firm won't show up for searches such as:

- Free lawyer
- Crash lawyer for motorcycle accidents
- Personal injury lawyer
- Should I hire a crash lawyer?

If a searcher misspells the keywords in your ad, it won't show up. This is the downside of using exact match keywords while it can help you avoid wasting impressions, it also means you might miss out on potential opportunities. Remember that people often use unconventional terms or spell words differently, so you could miss valuable traffic. That brings us to the next match type.

Phrase Match

Enter your keyword in straight quotation marks. People will see your ad when they type in the keyword in that precise order, but your ad will also display if they type additional words before or after: "Motorcycle Crash Lawyer"

With this keyword match type, here are some of the searches where your ad will appear:

- Best Motorcycle Crash Lawyer
- Motorcycle Crash Lawyer Near Me
- Motorcycle Crash Lawyer in Kansas City
- Motorcycle Crash Lawyer Consultation

However, your ad will not appear if the search includes anything between the keywords or uses them in a different order. For example:

- Crash Motorcycle Lawyer
- Lawyer for Motorcycle Crash
- Lawyer in Kansas City for Motorcycle Crash

For your law firm, I recommend using "phrase match" for your Google ads campaign. So, you will need to go back to your Excel sheet and add straight quotation marks to your keywords.

Negative Keywords

Once you have added your straight quotation marks to your keyword list, the next step you need to take is to create your negative keyword list. This step is crucial to improving your click-through rate and overall Quality Score.

Be careful with this, though. One wrong move and your entire campaign could suffer. So, initially, run your Google ads with no negative keywords. Then, after a couple of weeks, check back with your campaign and see if any keywords you are not happy with trigger your ads. If you completed the step above correctly, you shouldn't have to spend much time on this.

Once you have your keywords list, copy and paste it into the keyword box.

Step #10: Creating The Ads

The most important thing to remember when creating your Google ads is to ensure when your target customer sees your ad, they think to themselves, "Hey! This advertisement is for me!" Remember, these people are already looking for solutions to their problems. So keep it simple, and create the ads to show you are the expert who can solve their problem.

Here are two ads that appeared when I searched for "Semi - Truck Accident Lawyers."

With Justice For All - The Local Firm - 50+ Attorneys

https://have-a-case.abclawyer.com/

For More Than 40 Years, ABC Law Has Provided Trusted Legal Care For Clients. Our Team of Accident Attorneys Have Recovered Over $1 Billion For Clients.

Semi-Truck Accident Lawyers - Talk To A Lawyer Today!

www.notsemitruckaccidentlawyers.com

Our law firm specializes in helping victims get the money they deserve.
Visit our website to learn about our law firm and our success with semi-truck accidents.

If I am searching for a semi-truck accident lawyer, I am choosing the second one. On top of that, the first advertisement's quality score is pitiful, making them pay more per click.
Before you move on, create 3-4 split tests of the advertisement.

Step #11: Landing Page

Before you click publish, you need to create your landing page. To ensure success with your landing page, it's important to consider the needs of both the Google editor and visitors. The Google editor will review your landing page to determine if it meets their guidelines, and if it does not, your ad may be disapproved, or your ads account may be suspended or banned.

Ensuring that your landing page meets Google's standards for a good user experience is crucial to avoid these issues.

According to Google, five main elements contribute to a positive landing page experience:

1. Relevant, useful, and original content closely related to your ad text and keywords.
2. Transparency and trustworthiness, including clear information about how you will use any personal data shared by visitors.
3. Easy navigation to help the visitors find what they are looking for quickly and easily.
4. Fast-loading pages to keep visitors engaged.
5. Mobile-friendliness, as over half of all traffic now comes from mobile devices. Therefore, it's best to design your landing page with mobile users in mind first and then optimize it for tablets and desktop computers.

I have created a Landing Page Checklist to ensure you follow Google's policies:

- **Aligns with the overall campaign.** Your landing page must align with your overall campaign, ensuring your quality score remains high. The headline and copy on your landing page should align with the text in your advertisement.
- **It is easy to understand what you offer.** If a Google employee reviews your landing page, what your business offers should be clear.
- **Trusted claims.** Make sure only to make claims that you can support with verifiable, third-party data, especially if you have a strong track record or have received positive reviews or awards.
- **Include testimonials.** Client testimonials are critical to the success of your landing page. We have

become a review-based society; the more social proof you have, the better. Put the testimonials near your call to action. You want as much firepower as possible near your CTA.

- **Website design.** Design is important for making a good first impression. Make sure to invest in a professional and well-designed page that is easy to navigate. Keep it simple and avoid outdated or userunfriendly design. Within the first few seconds of landing on your page, your prospect should feel that the content is relevant, valuable, and clear about the action they should take.

- **Privacy policy.** Have your privacy policy at the bottom of your landing page. It should be easy to find.

- **Contact information.** While it is not strictly required, Google prefers that you include your physical address (not just a P.O. box) on your site to help build trust and show that you are a legitimate business with a physical location. At a minimum, you should have a working phone number or functional email address available on your site.

- **Disclaimers.** Be prepared to include a disclaimer with your testimonials. Sometimes, Google may require a disclaimer next to each testimonial, depending on your industry. Alternatively, you can include a main disclaimer in your footer stating that "individual results may vary." This can help manage expectations and ensure your testimonials are not misleading.

The main goal of your landing page is to turn traffic into leads. Therefore, the better the landing page, the more leads you will generate from your Google ads. Here are the bullet points you need to remember when creating your landing page.

- The power of one. Only promote one service and offer one way to contact your firm.
- Keep it consistent. Your landing page needs to remain consistent with the verbiage in your advertisement.
- Established and Trustworthy. Show the visitors your law firm is established and trustworthy. Use client testimonials and show off your awards.

Setting up Conversion Tracking

Tracking your conversions is the single most important thing you can do. I am a numbers guy. I like to be able to go to my clients and say, "This month, we generated 34 form submissions from Campaign A and 44 form submissions from Campaign B. Here are their names and numbers. How many of these turned into paying customers?" This allows me to funnel more money into campaigns that perform well and pull back on those that do not.

Step #12: Launch Campaign

You are ready to launch your campaign with all the steps above completed. But, remember, this isn't the type of thing where you can set it and forget about it. You will need to come back and review this regularly.

I know that chapter was a lot. But, when Google ads are implemented correctly, they can generate outstanding results for your law firm. Unfortunately, most law firms don't understand the difference between a good and bad Google ads campaign. Here is a recap:

- **Quality score:** Most law firms' quality scores are pitiful!
- **Keywords:** Use "phrase match" or [exact match] to ensure you only pay for keywords you want to bid on.
- **Landing Page:** Build a landing page for the specific campaign with conversion tracking.
- **Conversion Tracking:** You must know how many conversions your Google ads generate for your law firm and how much each conversion costs you!

With your Google ads properly created, you can generate results you never thought possible. What basic premise will allow you to generate results with Google ads? Focus and discipline.

Now that your Google ads campaign is ready, let's move on to targeted marketing.

CHAPTER EIGHT: SOCIAL MEDIA MARKETING

The next step to growing your law firm is implementing targeting ads, such as social media, YouTube, and Display ads. Targeting ads are a form of cold outreach. You are interrupting or inserting your law firm while someone is engaged in another activity. Therefore, you must create something that piques their interest enough for them to take action on your advertisement. In this chapter, I will show you how to do just that. I will also show you how to follow up with them to convert them into a customer and build your Golden Egg.

Since platforms such as Facebook, Instagram, and YouTube change so often, I will give you the strategy to use when using these advertising mediums. When you implement this method, ensure that you have a training expert (such as myself) implement it for you!

Let's jump right in, starting with an Ethical Bribe.

CREATE AN ETHICAL BRIBE

An Ethical Bribe is a piece of content or information your target market would want in exchange for their name, email, and phone number. We are merely giving them something of value for their contact information.

Here is the main reason to create an Ethical Bribe. There is a very small chance you will generate a sale for your targeted advertisements. Generating clients from targeted advertising is a lot like how relationships start with the goal of getting married. You will have no chance if you get down on one knee and ask the person to marry you the first time you meet them.

But, if instead you ask them for their number, build the relationship, and eventually getting married is inevitable. (As long as you do everything else correctly.)

Recent studies suggest that before a prospect uses your company, they must see or hear from you seven to twelve times. You have started that connection when you can grab their information and contact them directly. You also won't have to keep paying "big tech" to get in touch with your potential clients, but more on that later.

You need to stand out from your competition by creating an Ethical Bribe that gives value to your target market and paints you as an expert. Something that they actually will want to read, rather than just getting boring information puked on them.

Become The Expert

Another benefit of creating Ethical Bribes is that you can paint yourself as an expert in your field. You become an expert by educating people and showing that you know what you are talking about. Becoming an expert is important because people want to deal with experts and are willing to pay much more for their services.

Your customers want to know that you completely understand your profession and can solve their problems perfectly.

Experts can charge what they want and bring on the best clientele.

Teach The Why, Sell The How

Another critical element that you can take advantage of with an Ethical Bribe is teaching *why* your target clientele needs your services and then selling them the solution, the *how*.

One of the biggest problems I see when taking on new clients is this: lawyers and their employees assume that their target market knows the benefits of using their firm. They skip over *why* they need you and preach *how* to hire you.

Some of the most common how selling is telling people how long you have been in business, how many employees you have, and how you are so much better than your competitor. Instead of telling them, show them. I live in Missouri, the Show Me State. Show me!

Most of the time, your target market has no idea how much your company can help them, and even if they do, remind them every chance you get. Show that you genuinely care about them and want their lives to improve. That is what business is truly all about.

Benefits and Features

When you are creating these Ethical Bribes, you must remember one thing. You are only trying to hit on the emotions (benefits) of using your law firm. Please don't create an Ethical Bribe that is packed with logic. This is speaking on the technical aspect of things.

Benefits are how the product or service will improve their lives. Your potential client always purchases everything twice, once in their head and then once from you.

Remember, the potential clientele thinks in pictures and is trying to imagine in their head all of the positive emotions they will feel once they finally buy your product or service. So help them as much as you can. Remember earlier in the book when I talked about personalization? Show them who you are and what to expect when they call your law firm. Dealing with lawyers is intimidating for a lot of the population. Show them there is nothing to be afraid of.

So, what are the different styles of Ethical Bribes you can use? Below are the most common types of Ethical Bribes I have found from The Conversion Code by Chris Smith:

1. **Guide/Report/eBook:** When you build a guide, report, or eBook, you can give your potential clients more perceived value. For example, when you take the time to create a guide on "The First Thing To Do If You Get A DUI," it increases conversions massively compared to a blog post!

2. **Cheat Sheets/Checklists:** People gravitate to quick wins and shortcuts.

3. **Toolkit/Resource list:** "The First 5 Steps You Need To Take If You Are Thinking About Getting A Divorce." Helpful content that is quick and easy to deliver.

4. **Webinar:** A webinar is an online class or discussion. People register for a spot, and you teach them through video.

Warning: If you promise value and do not fulfill your promise, your credibility is lost, and you can kiss the prospect goodbye. There is no second date for you! Going back to being able to stand out from your competition, look at all of the marketing messages today; it is usually something that looks like this:

XYZ Law Firm
Services we provide: Service A
Service B
Service C
Call for a free case evaluation!

This advertisement is boring and will not generate any kind of interest. You might as well light your marketing dollars on fire; it will probably generate more attention. Law firms are actually spending money on advertisements that look like this. No wonder they claim marketing "doesn't work!" This is your competition, and we will blow their asses out of the water!

We're only asking for a second date here, not going for the home run with our advertisements. That will come later. Your strategy needs to be infused with short-term tactics. When you take the time to create something that will add value to your target market's lives, you move from being just another law firm begging for attention to an expert in your field. Most consumers have never had a company add value to their lives before giving them money, only after.

Most companies are in a standoff with their potential customers. It's just like someone standing over a fire, saying, "I will give you more wood, but first, you must produce more heat!"

Let's look at an example of an Ethical Bribe for an Estate Planning Attorney.

"Free eBook: What will happen to your assets if something happens to you? Create an Estate Plan Based on Your Individual And Family's Needs.

As you age, your financial needs and health concerns naturally evolve.

Estate planning allows you to age comfortably by addressing changes and challenges head-on.

Get The FREE eBook Today!"

Is this the most riveting Ethical Bribe? No way. But it speaks to my client's target market. So if someone requests this, they are his target market, and we can begin our follow-up process.

Once you have information created for your Ethical Bribe, you need to hire a graphic designer to make it visually appealing. At WiseGuys, we create these all the time. So, if you need an amazing graphic designer for your Ethical Bribe, reach out, and my team will get it done at WiseGuysdm.com/contact.

Creating The Headline For The Advertisement

The headline is the starting point and most crucial part of every advertisement. When creating the headline, ensure it captures the attention of your target audience.

Opening with a Question

- Are you curious about...?
- Have you ever stayed up at night thinking about...?
- Do you ever ask yourself...?
- Are you secretly afraid of...?
- Looking for just the right...?
- Tired of empty promises from...?
- Tired of the same old...?

Opening with a Statement

- Let me ask you a simple question.
- We will change your mind about...

- It's not every day that...
- Here's an idea worth considering.
- Don't let ___ keep you from getting ahead.
- Don't be caught without ___.
- ___ often spells the difference between failure and success.
- If you are like most people, you probably...
- We live in an increasingly complex world.
- Today, more than ever...
- It's never too late to...
- Let's talk about why you need ___.
- Let's face it.
- Let's be honest.

Copy For The Advertisement

Almost every platform you run these ads on will have a spot to add a paragraph of text. Pack this with the benefits of reading and downloading your Ethical Bribe. But, again, this should only pique the interest of your target market. Riveting to your target market, boring to everyone else.

Graphic For Ad

The graphic for the advertisement should be the same image as your Ethical Bribe. Ensure the image is properly sized for the platform you are running it on and the graphic fits the target audience you are looking to generate leads from.

Platform To Use

My go-to platforms to run advertisements are Facebook and Google Display ads. Since Facebook owns Instagram, you can choose to run ads there too. Social media marketing is about creating that first interaction with the potential customer. You must remember that you are interrupting something they are doing, and if you don't come up with anything that will stop and catch their attention, you will be throwing money out the window. For Social Media Marketing, it is the same strategy no matter which platform you decide to use. Offer value, get their contact information, and close later.

I love testing my Ethical Bribe on Facebook because you can capture a lead without making them leave the platform. When you log in to the ads manager and click "create a new campaign," there will be an option for a lead generation campaign.

This is massive. You want your Target Market to get your Ethical Bribe quickly and easily. If you make them leave the platform they are on, your conversion rates will drop massively.

Landing Page To Convert

If you don't utilize Facebook, you will need to create a landing page for your traffic to receive your offer. I recommend at least testing your offer on Facebook to ensure your target market wants your Ethical Bribe before investing money in creating a landing page.

If you decide to make a landing page, follow the checklist outlined in the previous chapter!

Split Test & Budget

For your budget, start small and increase the amount of money in the ads, generating the best results. Simple as that. Every single advertisement that you make needs to have an A/B split test. The A/B split test creates the same advertisement but with different content.

You might have a video in advertisement A and a photo in

advertisement B. You are testing the waters to see what works and what does not.

I do split-testing ads to start any campaign, which has always produced excellent advertisements.

The first thing I do is create at least ten different variations of the same advertisement.

After that, I set them up in brackets just like they do in tournaments like March Madness. Then, finally, I launch all ten of them with a budget of something small, like $3/day.

After a couple of days, I check on the advertisements and see which ones performed better than their counterparts. The ad that did better got to move up the bracket, and the one that lost gets thrown out. Eventually, it makes it up to the finals, and whichever advertisement wins gets to run. After the ad runs for a while, the conversion rate may fall. If so, start the process over again!

There are a couple of different ways to measure the performance of an advertisement. It could be on the click-through rate, clicks to your landing page, or leads generated. Depending on how intense you are, you can make a bigger bracket and test as many advertisements as you want. The most I have seen was around 100 or so, which was insane, but they produced one of the best-performing advertisements I have seen to date.

The advertisement produces 20 to 30 leads daily, while the company spends less than 20 cents per lead. The more testing that you do, the better your advertisements will be.

How different would your law firm be if you brought on 2030 new leads daily?

Another big factor you must consider is that marketing is an investment; the more money you put in, the more you will get out. That being said, marketing is not gambling. Before you go all in, make sure that you see stable returns. If you see an advertisement working, throw more money at it. If you see an ad that has poor returns, shut it down.

MANAGING YOUR GOLDEN EGG

As your law firm grows, you will build your Golden Egg. This massive database is filled with your target market and past clients. So, how do you nurture and take care of this Golden Egg to ensure it provides value to your law firm for years to come? If done correctly, you will generate loyal followers who will never forget you. They will refer your law firm to friends and family, and you will always stay top of mind.

The first step that we must take in the conversion process is to nurture the prospect and continuously provide them with substantial value. As I said earlier, a lead takes around 8 to 12 follow-ups and interactions to become a paying customer. Simply put, the money is in the follow-up.

How many times, on average, do you think the typical business follows up with a lead before giving up? By the fourth contact, 89.8% of companies have given up. We're going to be different.

Conversion Basics

We must nurture the relationship before asking the prospect to use our company. We need them to get to know us more, and the best way to do this is by sending out consistent and valuable information.

You will need to employ a couple of components to give yourself the best chance of converting your leads into paying customers. First, to continue to nurture the prospect, we will need to add them to an email marketing campaign. You can use a couple of techniques when creating your email marketing campaign, but this is the most effective method I have used so far.

1. Nurturing Email
2. Nurturing Email
3. Nurturing Email
4. Sales Email

Ethical Bribe Delivery

Make sure this gets to them ASAP! Use automation tools to ensure that there is no lag time. The longer they wait, the harder it will be to turn them into clients. The subject of this email needs to be what they requested. Do not try to get fancy with this; there is no need. Keep it simple, and just make the subject bar the headline of your Ethical Bribe.

One thing that I have learned is that people prefer to avoid downloading items from the internet. Therefore, ensure your Ethical Bribe is the content of the email and give them the option to download it with a PDF attachment if they wish.

Remember to provide a quick and easy method for those who have requested your Ethical Bribe to contact you. Some may even book an appointment without reading it first. One way to simplify this process is by using a Calendly link.

After the Ethical Bribe is sent, how long do you wait to start the follow-up sequence? Remember, you have successfully got them to take an interest in you. That is the hard part; now, all you have to do is nurture them and eventually turn them into paying customers!

Nurturing Emails

Believe it or not, the content of your nurturing emails should already be created. Remember in chapter three when we talked about repurposing content? This is another place where you can use the content you have already created. You will take pieces of the webinar you created for your Nurturing emails and use them for your email marketing campaign.

Sales Email

Once you have sent three nurturing emails to your Golden Egg, you can send a sales email. Here is what the formula looks like for the sales email.

1. The problem they are having
2. How your law firm can solve their problems with your services
3. Describe how amazing their life would look with emotion after you solve this problem
4. Direct call to action or calendar link

Remember, most prospects won't use your company until the eighth contact, so don't get down on yourself if they don't convert immediately. Another critical aspect of email marketing is that you can keep in touch with your leads and past customers without paying "Big Tech."

Continuously growing this massive stockpile of your target clientele will be like sitting on a gold mine. However, before this stockpile turns into your own Golden Egg, you must ensure you are taking care of it and doing what is necessary for it to thrive. Once you do this, you can profit from it for years to come!

EMAIL MARKETING TIPS

Email Marketing will be one of the most important tools for your company in your quest to convert leads into paying customers. Therefore, Here are some additional tools to help you in the world of Email Marketing.

Tip #1: Every email you send needs to provide value to your leads.

Tip #2: One of the main reasons someone opens an email is the sender's name. Make sure you use either your first name or your business name. If your email is sent from the "Sales Team," it will likely not be opened.

Tip #3: Make sure all of your headlines pop. Bold claims or mysteries work best when trying to get opens for your email marketing campaigns.

Tip #4: Schedule and create emails at least two weeks in advance. Make sure you are consistent with the time and frequency of your campaigns.

Tip #5: Always make sure you are taking the time to grow your email list. For most of your potential and previous clientele, their email rules their lives. Email marketing is the best way to keep in touch with your prospects for free.

This process will allow your law firm to be seen as the expert for your niche. Once you have a solid plan for one niche, expand to another. Create a separate Ethical Bribe and email follow-up.

As I was writing this chapter, an attorney posted this on LinkedIn, and it conveyed the essence of this chapter.

"I started my law firm one year ago.

A few months later, I signed up a wrongful death case that was referred to me by an insurance agent.

My law partner and I met with the widow. During the consultation, the widow asked my law partner whether he remembered her...

Turns out, my law partner had represented the deceased and his widow 10+ years ago. My partner did an excellent job on the case. Why didn't the widow call my law partner and hire him for the wrongful death case?

She couldn't remember his name...

The moral of this story: Lawyers have to stay top of mind. Just doing a good job isn't enough. It's easier now than ever to stay top of mind. Make sure that your former clients think of you when they have a legal issue."

Attract your potential client's attention with Ethical Bribes, keep in touch with them through email marketing, and stand apart from your competition!

CHAPTER NINE: HIRING A DIGITAL MARKETING COMPANY

So, I am sure you are asking yourself, "When should I hire a digital marketing company?" Do you want to know my completely unbiased opinion? As soon as possible. However, you should take a few important steps to avoid any negative consequences before doing so.

The best way to hire a digital marketing company is to ask around and see which company other law firms use. For example, WiseGuys really only works with referrals these days. Very few digital marketing companies do amazing work, so when you are one of them, referrals come in abundance. You will never receive a robocall from me, and I will never send you an email promising backlinks. Why am I telling you all of this? Because the digital marketing companies that are good at what they do won't spam you with robocalls.

Below is a review I received from a client that illustrates the typical lifecycle law firms go through when choosing a digital marketing company.

"After hiring countless Gurus and growing tired of lighting tens of thousands of dollars on fire, I was introduced to Wise-Guys Digital Marketing by a fellow estate planning attorney.

We made the leap after being shown (with actual data) that our current SEO campaign wasn't cutting it. My only regret is not finding these guys sooner! A few months in, and we're already up 40% during our SLOW season! I'm excited about the opportunities this growth will provide us and look forward to working with this crew for all of our SEO, Google Ads, and digital advertising needs."

- Michael Jenkins; Jenkins & Jenkins, Estate Planning Attorneys.

During my meetings with law firms, I frequently hear about their experiences with digital marketing firms. Many have spent significant amounts of money with little to no return on investment, leading them to switch to a different firm and repeat the process. Here are some things to consider when selecting a digital marketing company to avoid this cycle.

First and foremost, if it sounds too good to be true, it probably is. There is no such thing as something for nothing.

Here are the things you need to do to ensure you won't get taken for a ride by a less-than-average digital marketing company.

- Since you are just starting your law firm, will they adjust their pricing to ensure they can grow with you?
- Do they show you previous work and case studies? Ask them about their process (data should be mentioned.)
- Look at their reviews
- Do they insist on locking you into year-long contracts?
- Do they have people vouching for them?

- Are they transparent about their pricing? Every law firm is different. The price they charge should vary based on the competition and the goals you want to achieve. If they have packages that don't vary, be suspicious.
- Do they ask about your law firm's goals and objectives? All of our plans are built around this. If they don't ask, it is very hard to build the roadmap.

My motto: Trust but verify. Talk is cheap.

CHAPTER TEN: LAW FIRM GROWTH CHECKLIST

WiseGuys Proven Process For Growing Law Firms

I created this checklist to help you grow your law firm.

1. Getting Started

- Are you thinking like a lawyer or a business person?
- Sales, Sales, Sales
- Patience and persistence

2. Niche

- Have you identified the niche you can dominate?
- Are you in a city/area you want to dominate? Have you performed market research to confirm this is a good choice?
- Have you created a USP to stand apart from your competitors using the One Star Improvement Plan or Groups Method?

3. Website

- Have you identified the keywords you want your website to rank for?
- Optimized website pages? (Title, H1, and H2 tags, to name a few.)
- Can you provide a walkthrough of what it's like to work with your law firm?
- Is it built to convert traffic into leads?
- Is it easy to contact your law firm? (The phone number is in the top right corner.)
- Is it written so Google can understand it? (NLP)
- Does it have personalization? (Photos of you and your firm.)
- Compelling "About Us" page
- Does it have at least 50 pages written for SEO?
- Do you write and upload a blog once a month?
- Do you cover each service you offer in great detail? (Topical Authority)
- Is it fast and mobile-friendly?
- Does it show the visitor you are the expert? (Webinars, Books, Educational Content)
- Does it have at least 20 client testimonials? (Video if possible)

4. Google Business Profile

- Have you claimed your Google Business Profile?
- Are you posting on your GBP once a week?
- Have you added photos of the interior and exterior of your office?
- Have you added all the correct information, such as your website, physical address, and phone number?
- Are you adding photos to your GBP once a week?

- Are you getting *at least* three Google reviews a week? (Ask friends and family if you are just starting out.)
- Have you replied to all of your reviews?
- Have you added all of your services and detailed descriptions to your services tab?
- Have you added all of your products to the products tab?
- Have you chosen the correct business category?
- Have you added your appointment link?
- Have you confirmed your business hours?
- Have you enabled the chat feature?
- Have you asked yourself and answered FAQ's on your profile?
- Have you written a business description with your main keyword(s) and city?
- Have you allowed messages to be sent through your profile?

5. Expert Status & Content Creation

- Are you creating guides and checklists to show your clients you are the expert?
- Are you leveraging your time? (Create once, use forever)
- Do you show your clients why you are an expert?
- Can you host webinars? Record them and add them to your social media and website.

6. Local SEO

- Have you run a Local Search Audit for your law firm recently?
- Does your law firm have at least 150 name, address, phone number citations?

- Are important directories such as Apple Maps, Yelp, and Bing Local claimed?
- Is your Google Business Profile embedded into the footer of your website?
- Is the business information on your website the same as your Google Business Profile?
- Are you getting reviews on platforms such as Yelp and Bing Local?

7. Google Ads

- Run Google Ads while your organic rankings are increasing
- Are your Google ads set up correctly?
- Do you have a landing page to convert the ads?
- Are you keeping track of your Cost Per Acquisition?

8. Offline Marketing

- Are you involved with your community?
- Can you sponsor events that your target market attends?
- Are you growing your network on LinkedIn?
- When someone refers you, does your online presence show your potential customer you are the law firm for the job?
- Has everyone in your law firm taken a course on sales?

While the methods of growing law firms are always evolving and changing, these core principles will allow your firm to grow.

BONUS CHAPTER-MARKETING SECRETS OF THE ULTRA-WEALTHY

CHAPTER ONE: BEGIN WITH THE END IN MIND

"Let others get caught up in the twist and turns of the everyday battle, relishing their little victories. Grand Strategy will bring you the ultimate reward: the last laugh."
-Robert Greene, 48 Laws Of Power

What qualities do some of the most successful humans and companies have that all others don't? You see, success leaves clues, and it is our job as humans to pick up on these clues and act upon them, evolve. If we didn't evolve, we would still be in caves, living off the land, competing with the rest of the animal kingdom. Is it by chance or luck that since the dawn of time, every single successful group or entity has followed the same pattern—no matter how large or small? No.

From Alexander the Great down to the modern-day corporation, they all have one thing in common. They understood their Grand Strategy and had the grit to complete what they set their minds to, the one end goal they are striving to achieve. So the question is, why do some people ignore these clues? Wouldn't it be easier if they just follow what works, or is it merely that that just have no idea? Are they truly that oblivious, or is it something else?

To gather some context, we need to step back and understand how humans separated from the rest of the animal kingdom in the first place. In Robert Greene's book, The 33 Strategies of War, he says, "Thousands of years ago, we humans elevated ourselves above the animal world and never looked back. Figuratively speaking, the key to this evolutionary advance was our powers of vision: language and the ability to reason that it gave us, let us see more of the world around us. To protect itself from a predator, an animal depending on its senses and instincts; it could not see around the corner, or to the other end of the forest.

"We humans, on the other hand, could map the entire forest, study the habits of dangerous animals and even nature itself, gaining deeper, wider knowledge of our environment. We could see the dangers coming before they were here. This expanded vision was abstract: where an animal is locked in the present, we could see into the past and glimpse as far as our reason would take us into the future. Our insight expanded further and further into time and space, and we came to dominate the world."

This is the key that I want you to see. Very few people nowadays utilize this fantastic tool that got us here in the first place—drifting wherever the wind takes them, no direction at all.

"In a world where people are increasingly incapable of thinking consequently, more animal than ever, the practice of grand strategy will instantly elevate you above others."
-Robert Greene

Our strength is not that we are the fastest or the strongest in the animal kingdom. Our power is that we are able to see what we want, create a plan on how to get there, and get it done. Building on past mistakes and learning from them.

This is nothing new. This is how humans survived and evolved. We were able to have vision, and we were able to plan tactics and strategies to get us out of harmful situations before they happened. This is how we were able to control the animal kingdom completely. This is why we dominate the sky, land, and ocean.

Even with this extraordinary strength that God blessed humanity with, we find ourselves in bad situations. Society got too comfortable. Life is now too easy compared to our primal days. We no longer have to worry about a saber tooth tiger entering our cave in the middle of the night.

How was Alexander The Great able to conquer the entire Persian Empire before the age that most of us are allowed to have a beer? From birth, his mother gave him a clear destiny and goal: to rule the known world. From the age of three, he could see in his mind's eye the role he would play when he was thirty. He was trained to master his emotions, and understood the tactical moves he must make. He always was thinking ahead, saying to himself, "This action will advance me toward my goal; this one will lead me nowhere."

He had a Grand Strategy, and once he had that, he developed tactical objectives to get there, and then everything else fell into place. He also had excellent teachers that helped him along the way.

When you are trying to grow your company, there is a system in place, a solid plan that has already worked for centuries. All you have to do is follow it. Starbucks has a Grand Strategy, "To inspire and nurture the human spirit – one person, one cup, and one neighborhood at a time." Every move Starbucks makes, they can look back and ask themselves, "Will this action move us toward our goal, or away from it?"

That's it. That is the exact method that every single

successful person or organization took to achieve victory. They established a clear Grand Strategy and then took steps to achieve the goals, but seeing where you want to end up is the easy part.

So why do some people ignore these clues? Wouldn't it be easier if they just follow what works? Are they indeed that oblivious, or is it something else? As the saying goes, "If it were more information we needed, we would all be rich and have six-packs." The information is here, and it's always been here.

I believe that what separates the great companies, people, and organizations is having the grit to see it all the way through. They make the right moves consistently. When you make a long-term plan, you must have a lot of patience and resilience to see it through. At a certain point, you know that eating your body weight in cake is not a good idea, but that is your future self's problem, not yours.

Humans are in love with instant gratification. They want happiness now, even though it will prove to be detrimental down the road. Truly great leaders are able to understand that nothing comes easy, and if it did, everyone would do it.

I can tell within five minutes if a potential client has the grit to implement this strategy. Are they looking for a get rich quick scheme, or are they looking to dominate their industry? There is nothing wrong with wanting a get rich quick scheme, but this is not where you will find it.

Before you start this journey, ask yourself, "Am I in for the long haul, or not?" If you are, get ready for the ride of your life. You might be asking yourself, "Can I really use this method to grow my company?"

My answer is this:

- Humans have used the Grand Strategy to...
- Dominate the Animal Kingdom

- Harness Electricity
- Communicate via Radio Frequencies
- Visit the Moon
- Discover Break Through Medical Treatments And much, much more. Yes, I know it will work to grow your company. I'll also walk you through the exact way to build your foundation and guide you through every tactical step you must take to achieve your Grand Strategy. I'm going to give you the magic formula. Bold claim? You bet.

I can show you how to establish your foundation and employ tactics to get to your desired end goal, but at the end of the day, it's up to you to take action. It's as simple as that.

There are three main aspects of creating a Grand Strategy.

1. Identify Grand Strategy
2. Establish Foundation
3. Establish Tactical Rocks

First Step: Identify Grand Strategy

- $15,000,000 in revenue in 5 years?
- #1 Supplier in the Country by 2026?
- Bring your product to every household in America?
- Every household in the world?

The first step is to choose where you want to go. What is your overall mission for your company? What is the end goal? When you are lying on your death bed, what would have to happen for you to be completely satisfied? Let's assume that there is such a thing.

I want your Grand Strategy to be so massive that it scares you a little bit when you say it. When you can see it in your mind and honestly believe that it is possible, that is when your life will never be the same!

The Man Who Thinks He Can
Poem by Walter D. Wintle

If you think you are beaten, you are
If you think you dare not, you don't,
If you like to win, but you think you can't
It is almost certain you won't.
If you think you'll lose, you're lost
For out of the world we find,
Success begins with a fellow's will
It's all in the state of mind.
If you think you are outclassed, you are
You've got to think high to rise,
You've got to be sure of yourself before
You can ever win a prize.
Life's battles don't always go
To the stronger or faster man,
But soon or late the man who wins
Is the man who thinks he can.

Choose your Grand Strategy, then commit to it. Commit 100% to everything in life, no matter what. The grass is not greener on the other side, trust me.

Second Step: Foundation

The second step we are going to take is to set up a proper foundation. Think about it in this context. Imagine that your Grand Strategy is on the other side of a rushing river. Swimming is not an option. We will build a foundation so that the slippery rocks that we step on won't slide out from underneath us. The rocks you're stepping on to get across the river are your tactical rocks. If you do a superficial job or don't build a foundation at all, you will eventually slip, fall in the river, and die. Rather than you actually dying, it is your dreams, goals, and desires. Personally, I'd rather die than give up on my dreams, goals, and desires. How about you?

Third Step: Tactical Rocks

Now that we understand where we want to go and have the foundation in place, we will develop the steps to get there—one step at a time, with purpose and determination. I'm going to walk you through the exact steps I take with my clients to achieve their desired Grand Strategy for business growth.

Remember, most companies these days are only focusing on the tactical side of things, acting more and more like animals. They are either too lazy or are simply unaware of linking their Grand Strategy. Without the link, you are dead in the water.

Without understanding your Grand Strategy, you will have no idea where you need to go, and eventually, you will get tired and fall into the river. Without establishing the foundation, you will be running in quicksand and eventually get so tired and frustrated you will lay down and die. When you use tactical marketing, you rely on small wins that bring very little long-term success. When you only rely on small tactical victories without a Grand Strategy, you will get lost and ultimately fail. Companies that "cook the books" so that their earnings calls look good are tactical players. They only think of short-term wins, even though the inevitable is coming.

Examples of tactical marketing are slashing your prices, competing solely on price, and using inaccurate sales methods to convince the client that your product or service does something that it does not. When you lie and cheat to get ahead, it will eventually all come crashing down!

Not all companies that just use tactical marketing are bad! Some companies simply do not know the difference. They were told, "Get the most customers in the door by any means necessary!" If this is you, don't worry. This is the new normal for companies. Humans are now so obsessed with instant gratification that they'd rather chose the easy way out rather than taking the time and really create something beautiful. Truly sad.

When you use tactical marketing skills without a long-term strategy, it is like a person with an addiction doing whatever they can to get their next "hit." The more you do it, the harder it is to get off it, just like being addicted to gambling.

This is what you need to be very aware of. If all you did was lose at the casino, they would have no clientele, so they plan the customer's experience flawlessly. While I was sitting in Las Vegas, I decided to watch one guy. He was very particular about which machine he picked. I overheard him talking to his buddy that he wanted to find one that someone had been at for a while. I thought it kind of made sense. The machine would be closer to handing out a big payday.

After a lady that had been sitting there for a while got up, he promptly sat down and deposited his crisp $100 bill. After about 15 pulls, he was down $55, and then bang! The machine started making all of these loud noises, and colors were lighting up all around him. As people looked over to his machine to watch this lucky fellow, a grin grew across his face like he was the chosen one. He had the Midas touch, simple as that. I even found myself smiling. I mean the colors and sounds; it was infectious! He was now up to $223, and I thought to myself, that's it? After the show that machine put on, I thought he might have won the whole damn casino!

But I continued to watch him after about thirty pulls; he was at about $177. Still not bad! Up $77 in Vegas! A strange thing started to happen, the wins got smaller, and the losses got bigger until he was at a depressing $3.53. As he hit the "cash-out" button, I asked myself why didn't he stop when he was at $223?

Here is the reason—as a human, your brain produces chemicals for pleasure. Two of those chemicals are dopamine and serotonin (more on serotonin later). Dopamine gets pumped into the brain for short term wins, like eating chocolate, hitting the jackpot at the casino— basically getting a quick victory. Dopamine is the part of the brain connected with addiction and what casinos take advantage of to create a loyal customer base.

When you are growing your company, it might feel good getting a client with false advertising or bringing on a client even though your company isn't truly going to solve their needs. It feels good to bring in five new clients even though you needed fifteen to break even. Remember, you are only hurting yourself even though it feels incredible at the moment.

When you use strategic and tactical marketing simultaneously, you will be able to charge what you want and not only be respected in your field but dominate it. The strategic marketing outlook will take a bit more planning, but it will bring massive results in the long term. Now that you understand your Grand Strategy, the rest of this book will show you how to get there.

While I was writing this book, Elon Musk sent out a tweet of his Grand Strategy of what he wanted to achieve back in 2006. It's simple. He knew where he wanted to go. Now all he had to do is figure out how to get there. He had his foundation and Grand Strategy, and that is genuinely all you need. Luckily for you, I am going to give you the step by step tactical plays as well.

<u>Elon 2006:</u>
the master plan is:

1. Build sports car
2. Use that money to build an affordable car
3. Use *that* money to build an even more affordable car
4. While doing above, also provide zero emission electric power generation options

You Will Need Gas

Before we move onto the next chapter, I want to hit on something that I feel many people struggle with when they achieve success, and that is suppressing their dark side. They tell themselves that wanting a great life is selfish, but it's not. Since you were a kid, you were told false prophecies about money and success, and it's B.S. You're supposed to live an abundant and fruitful life. Do not let small-minded people take that away from you.

In Tim S. Grover's book Relentless, he does a fantastic job explaining it this way, "You know the story of Dr. Jekyll and Mr. Hyde? A respected, upstanding doctor discovers a potion that temporarily turns him into a dark, sinister predator, and for a while, he finds he enjoys being free from fear and morality and emotions, not caring about anyone or anything. For the first time in his life, he does what he feels, not what he's been taught."

Welcome to the dark side. I want you to unmask this fabricated persona that society made you put on. I want you to be free and enjoy everything you want to enjoy. Eat whatever you want to eat, travel wherever you want, be yourself, and listen to your heart.

Do you know the people who made the rules? Most likely losers. These might be people that didn't mean you any harm.

They just might not know better themselves. They just listened to their parents and accepted it as reality.

A couple of years ago, I told one of my buddies that I was going to start a business.

His 29-year-old brother that still lived in their parents basement overheard me and said, "Ah, are you sure? There is a lot of things that could go wrong. Most businesses go bankrupt in the first year!"

I paused for a minute and asked him, "How do you know? Have you ever done it?"

Of course, he hadn't. He got all defensive and gave me one of those generic "good luck's" as most people do when you tell someone a big goal that they truly deep down wish they could do, but they don't because it scares them. They are too worried about what their friends and family would say.

One of my favorite questions to ask is, "How do you know?" Followed by, "Have you ever done it?"

Staple these questions into your memory every time someone wants to unload a heaping pile of B.S. on your dreams. Want to become a millionaire? Don't take advice from your broke aunt. Want to own real estate? Do not take advice from your loser friends. Want to grow a business? Ah, you get my point.

On this journey, you'll be faced with people that will criticize or be flat-out rude to you about your plans or goals. Here's how to deal with this. Don't get upset.

Keep a calm head and reply with, "I am sorry, but I don't take criticism from people I wouldn't take advice from," and leave it at that.

Why am I saying all of this? Because even the fastest sports cars need gas. You need to have the motivation to see this thing through. You are about to change the world. Not only does your future family need you, but the world also needs you. The world needs hope!

I believe in you, and I trust that you will make this world a better place. Some people don't like seeing someone go after their goals because that just reminds them of the ones they gave up on. Stand in the face of criticism, doubt, hatred, and fear and come out victorious.

"Success Requires No Explanation, Failure Permits No Alibis."
-Napoleon Hill, Author of Think and Grow Rich

Remember, the only difference between the successful human and the unsuccessful human is this: the successful human can see the bigger picture and create a plan to achieve their goals.

ABOUT THE AUTHORS

Cooper Saunders is the owner and founder of WiseGuys Digital Marketing, located in Kansas City, Missouri. He has worked with companies across the United States to grow their revenue and increase their brand visibility. Simply put, he knows how to grow businesses with tried and true marketing methods, developed by analyzing some of the world's most successful companies.

Miller Leonard has practiced law in three states and opened two law firms. He has practiced in the government, with small firms, and he loves to teach and share information.

Made in United States
Troutdale, OR
12/04/2024

25758146R00066